# You're Never To... to Save the Planet

Misha Herenger

Illustrated by Daniel DelValle

Rigby®

A Harcourt Achieve Imprint

www.Rigby.com
1-800-531-5015

I think about the environment a lot.
I worry that pollution is hurting
our planet.

I always remind Dad not to leave
the refrigerator door open.
An open refrigerator wastes energy.

I tell Mom we can walk to the post office
so she doesn't have to buy as much gas.

The truth is, both Mom and Dad do a lot to help the planet.
On Saturdays, Dad leads nature walks to teach people about the environment.
On Sundays, Mom volunteers at a recycling center.

I wanted to help, but I was too young
to work at the recycling center or to lead
nature walks.
I knew there must be something kids like me
could do.

Then one day I saw an Internet site
about a special group.
It's called Kids for a Clean Environment,
or Kids F.A.C.E.
It was just what I was looking for!

A nine-year-old girl
named Melissa started
the group.
She wanted to help
the planet.

At first her group had
just six members.
Now it has more than
300,000 members!
It's the biggest kids'
environmental group
in the world.

Melissa

When my Mom and I looked at the group's web site, we found lots of great volunteer ideas.

My favorite ideas:

 • Help plant trees.

 • Organize groups to pick up trash.

• Teach younger kids at school about recycling.

I was most curious about trees.
I wanted to learn why trees are so important.

At the Kids F.A.C.E. web site, I found out that people and animals depend on trees. Trees give us oxygen to breathe. The oxygen from trees also helps clean the air.

trees in New York City

Trees help cool the planet.
They give us shade.
They also take water from the ground and then put it back into the air.
This water becomes rain.

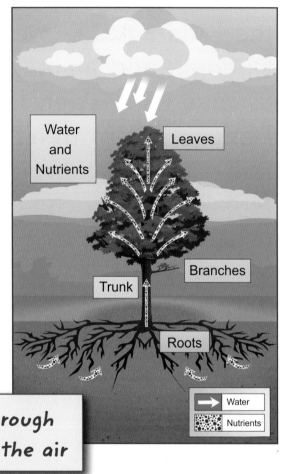

Water
and
Nutrients

Leaves

Branches

Trunk

Roots

Water
Nutrients

water going through trees and into the air

We cut down trees
to use their wood.
We burn some kinds
of wood to keep warm.
We also use some kinds
of wood to build new
houses and to make
other things, like baseball
bats and paper.

We need wood, but
we also need live trees
to help keep the
planet healthy.

I decided I really wanted to plant trees to replace the ones cut down. Kids F.A.C.E. sent me information about how to do it.

First I had to get trees to plant. I asked some stores to give us some trees. They said yes!

I planned a party called Tree-apalooza.
Then I needed to find some help.
I made posters and put them up
all around town.

Lots of kids signed up to help.
When the big day came,
we planted 200 trees all over town!

My new friends and I have already planned
our next event.
We're going to call it Trash the Litter Day!

Mom and Dad think we should slow down
a little bit.
"You don't have to save the whole planet
right now.
You're only nine years old," Mom tells me.

But I say, "Why wait?"